Also by Laura Kasischke:

POETRY:
Where Now: New and Selected Poems (Copper Canyon 2017)
The Infinitesimals (Copper Canyon 2014)
Space, in Chains (Copper Canyon 2011)
Lilies Without (Copper Canyon 2012)
Gardening in the Dark (Ausable 2004)
Dance and Disappear (U. of Massachusetts 2002)
What it Wasn't (Carnegie Mellon 2000)
Fire & Flower (Alice James 1998)
Housekeeping in a Dream (Carnegie Mellon, 1994)
Wild Brides (New York University Press 1990)

FICTION:
Mind of Winter (Harper Collins 2014)
The Raising: A Novel (Harper Collins 2011)
If a Stranger Approaches You (Sarabande, 2008)
Eden Springs (Wayne State University 2010)
In a Perfect World (Harper Collins 2009)
Feathered (Harper Collins 2009)
Boy Heaven (Harper Collins 2009)
Be Mine (Harcourt 2007)
The Life Before Her Eyes (Harcourt 2002)
White Bird in a Blzzard (Hyperion 1999)
Suspicious River (Houghtin Mifflin 1996)

THE TIME MACHINE

by Laura Kasischke

Acme Poem Company
Willow Springs Books
Spokane, Washington

Cataloging and Publication Information available from the Library of Congress on request.

Cover Art: Thomas Doyle
Cover Design: taylor d. waring
Interior Layout: taylor d. waring

FIRST EDITION

Willow Springs Books, Spokane, WA 99202

Printed in the United States of America

Printed by Gray Dog Press
ISBN: 978-0-9990050-5-7

willowspringsbooks.org

The Time Machine is Volume 10 in the Acme Poem Company Surrealist Poetry Series.

CONTENTS

The Time Machine was left
deserted on the turf
among the rhododendrons.

H.G. Wells

Perhaps

this is what it feels like
to be a woman
who is also a vulture. To be

a vulture
who is a woman
with a broken wing.

To have been
cared for by a mother.
To have hatched.
To have been featherless

as girl. To have been fed
the death
of someone else
by a mother
in a nest. And then

to have grown feathers. To
have been sent
out on her own. Not

to have wanted to go.
But to have flown.

To have
already known

the scent so well
she could smell it
as herself.

Two Canoes

Look: I'll show you again. There she is. Tied to a dock, aging at the end of a rope. Or lost in open water. What's the difference? The stars glint overhead like fish. The fish, like stars, swim under and around her, silver & finned & wriggling in their skins. Yes. Look: these writhing stars have been slipped into the whole idea of fish, except that fish...well, their flesh was zipped up far too hastily, too clumsily, for this. If you try to hold one to your face and kiss it like a slap, you'll understand. Since—

Since it's not a fish. It is the muscle plucked from the arm of a strong man as he paddles, or takes a swig from a flask, or takes a swing with a bat. You thought you could hold a thing like that? Well, the next time you forget what it's like to lie down with impulse such as this, close your eyes. Look: I'll show you again.

Secrets

A bear eating various bald vegetables in a cage off the freeway
next to a gas station. You
saw this as a child. Patches of raw flesh. A desperate loneliness.

You can live with such a thing most days, as well as your
neighbor who ran over
his daughter's cat. He
confessed it to you, weeping, begging
you to keep his secret, since
he told his wife and children that the cat
had run away, apparently
unhappy, looking for a better place.

You watched his little girl staple
posters—LOST CAT—to every
telephone pole in the neighborhood, and promised
you'd call her if you saw her cat.
Can you live with that?

Of course you can.

But one dark night
a new
comet appeared in the sky—some

streaming, speeding ball of dust and ice. Your husband
put on his jacket, went outside. You

didn't, never
wanting to have to think
about a thing like that
in some future you preferred
not to imagine. So

you stayed inside, and when
he came back to bed, so excited, you

wouldn't even let him describe it.

Beautiful Classmate from the Past

This beautiful classmate from the past who sat in front of me in math...

Every day for an hour and a half I watched the pale waterfall of her hair fall so smoothly it frightened us all.

I coughed, and scratched, had menstrual pain, attempted to swallow an aspirin without a sip of water, and when I choked, raised my hand, Mr. Nestor pointed to me and nodded because, although he tried to hide it out of kindness, he could never remember my name. Who could see me behind this beautiful classmate from the past?

Her hair, that—

Laziness of her hair—not a hair out of place, as they say—and the exposed perfection of her face, like the blinding idea God originally had before Eve fell so awkwardly from grace, before, finally, Satan had an even better idea:

To hide his womanly wiles inside the phallic symbol of a snake. Now:

How amazing that she, too, has grown
older, as we aged.
Because she has! Here

she is on Facebook. Not yet even dead! This
ongoing elevator—

which glides, silently, it seems, this elevator between the floors of a very tall tower, all day, of course, but also all night, it seems, although no one is inside it.

But, in its emptiness, still, something must always be riding, must always be there in the emptiness, just along, just for the ride—

Which I consider, along with this classmate, as I gaze today into the glass case in which a preserved girl is laid out for exhibit, plucked from a crypt, along with the three items excavated with her:

1) a shard of pottery

2) a blue bead

3) the skull of a delicate bird she'd recently eaten—a fact learned from her stomach when it was opened to reveal her terrible secret scrap of songbird as undigested meat.

Moonlanding

Forgot my helmet. My suit. My oxygen tank. My boots. They
were exasperated. Couldn't find my keys. My purse. I guess

I left that in the car, must be on the passenger seat. My
iPhone. My bright experience. My blissful

wave through space. They said, "You have to stay
inside the capsule. We'll be back." I asked them why. They said,

"Gravity: there isn't any." But then I told them about an old
lady who sat next to me once on the subway long ago, when

I was only twenty-four or so, who told me, "Not a leaf, and not
a stream, just space reflecting meaning, which is

your memory, which you

begin to lose, but not
until you no longer need it."

A Girl's Guide to Color

Do you remember pleasure?
Your favorite sweater?
A flattering scarf, a smart
cap, a pair of stones

dangling from your earlobes?

What color was it?

There are certain colors we all want to touch
on the right girl at the right time. But great

care must be taken. Short-
waisted, short-legged? From

your hemline to your hat you must wear a single shade.

Plump?
Break it up. A bright
coat. Orange
belt. If

your complexion's ruddy: no green for you, and don't

forget—the darker the dress, the smaller and smaller
it will make you. Pastels, however, enlarge and age
you. Either

take advantage of this, or avoid it at all costs.

And, as gold is strictly for brunettes, dirty
blondes must not wear blue. Another

rule: lilac, coral, and chartreuse. And

O, unlucky redhead, so many colors not for you.

Have you ever seen a sunset
clash with the sea or the sky?

Such is a redhead
in a yellow blouse
to the naked eye, and yet

so many girls make such mistakes
without ever knowing why, while

others seem as if they hardly
need to try. Witness

Cynthia, enchanting in her purple suit, high-
lights in her copper hair:

Cynthia would never wear rose and green together!
In fact, she's sewn this skirt herself—knowing
as she knows instinctively so

many things—that there are lovely bits
and pieces of everything, and that
a girl can't simply buy these. She

needs to learn to make them for herself.

Take Cynthia as your model, then—and
as she has done, if
you need chiffon,
get yards and yards of it at once, and then
divide it up among
all the girls in your club.

18 | And when you one day stumble upon
those girls, wearing
your chiffon, do not be jealous of them.

Do the stained
glass windows of Westminster Abbey
begrudge one another their radiance as
the sun passes from one to the other?

It's natural to be nothing, to become it. Just

do the best you can with what you have for
as long as you manage to have it, and

try always to remember how a color can
influence the mood of any man
who looks in its direction—and

knowing this, as you know now, decide
early in your life, would you rather

be a little jenny wren in winter-berry red, or
a parrot
in a crate
stowed below
the ship's deck? Our

friend Kiki was born without a sense
of color, but
she has a sparkling laugh, and that's

all some girls will ever
need: wearing the dumpy
uniforms of their class, and

still be a joy to see. But

let's be honest, shall we?
Which girl would you rather be—
Cynthia
or Kiki?

Would you paint the robes of the Virgin Mary
the red and black of a cancan dancer, or—?

This list grows longer as you grow older, but
you'll find it's
easy to memorize, and then
impossible to forget:

Too tall? Brown
jacket. Big hips? Never
a corsage of daffodils.
Are you a blocky girl?
If so, think
always of the cool
depths of Alpine
lakes. Flat-
chested? Avoid

the sky, the grass, the Pacific or Atlantic, as well
as any other great expanse, and you'll
be fine, most likely. Only

a few such simple principles, and
once you understand them, you'll
never need to crouch down and hold your

arms across your chest to hide your breasts again.
Or a hand between your legs to cover that. Have

you ever seen a maple tree in autumn try to disguise
the red of the leaves on its branches? Have—?

Of course you haven't.

Now the men are almost done.

Admittedly, it's an odd
era in which to be a girl. So many options—

and not just fashion.
When they slam the door and toss you a towel, perhaps

you should feel grateful. (Do you?) When

one shouts, Quit
crying, slut—you

should probably do as he says:

Clean yourself up, Kiki.
Cynthia, you're lucky we didn't cut you.

Someday, you may feel blessed. For

now it might be best just
to get off the floor, get dressed.

The Nose

Mystical, bifurcated rose. This
leftover clay
out of which we were shaped, stuck

in the middle of our faces. The gods, looking down, took
pity on us. This

will not be like a breast, or a wing, but they
will need something with which
to find their way home, to smell their babies, to locate
the emotions they've buried.

My father, waiting for me at the door, kissing me goodnight:
You've been smoking, drinking, or
you are foam
washed up with the tide
on the shore. Beer

spilled all over my good coat.

The Whole Point

Again today, each thing's
busy inventing the whole
point of itself. The sun,
whiskery with fire, burns.
The fish, predictabilities,
swim. Downstairs, some-
one fiddles with the knob
on the radio: Handel,
Johnny Cash, Handel,
Johnny Cash. The oxygen
in the tank, and on
the table, the syringe. The
tape, the gauze, the diligent
dog, barking reliably
at each passing car. Again
and again and again. My
son laces his shoes
in the threshold. My
cat curls around himself
like a breath in a chair. My
husband opens the door
and says, "Anyone home?
I'm home?" These
questions questioning
themselves. These cells replicating
themselves. Two mirrors reflecting
their own reflections. Or those
directions, so complex, they required
their own directions. The known
and unknown. I'm
taken out of this photo.

Like the woman
who answers the answer hotline
to ask why it is I want to know, and
both of the voices on each
end of the line
is my own.

Like seeing the archaeologist
with her knees in my ashes, to hear
her exclaim in
excited wonder
over my buttons and my bones.

What This Is

This is the decayed woman
in a beautiful blouse—
silk and ruffles and watercolor flowers.

The breeze in her sleeves.
The 1960s. The festivals
and lowlit parties. The recreational
derangement of those days. The goddesses'
blue eyelids. The noses crusted over
after the cold, the cry, the fight. What's

this?—how you live, how you die? Then
I see behind her, a girl walking into traffic, texting.
She looks up
when I honk—not grateful, not angry, not

even seeming startled
almost to have been
hit, or run over, by a moving vehicle, as if she knows

exactly what she's doing, and how
easily it could kill her, or how
it otherwise could be

the only way she'll ever
make it through this life, let alone across this street.

An Evil Meal

Like an evil meal being served to someone who hasn't eaten in many weeks...

Like veal, I suppose—the youngest and most tender of all meats, being, as it is, the flesh of a creature that only
once or twice managed to struggle onto its vague legs, smell the breeze, briefly wondering.

This world, an imagination locked into a calf-sized cage.

And the weasel with blood on its small, sweet face, darting across the field with the hen still held in its teeth.

But what is a weasel to do after stumbling upon an untended flock of deliciously flightless things? How lovely the little bits and pieces. How sweet, the eye socket, the marrow in the bones of their feet.

Such intricacy.

Whole cathedrals devoted to even more fleeting beliefs. In ancient cities, winding streets, leading to these beliefs.

Or the advertisements for things we begin to believe we need—teaching our children, as we ourselves were taught as children, that there's no difference between what we want and what we need. What we believed until we were told we didn't believe it.

Talisman

Little tin key
lost somewhere in my memory, returned to me in a dream.

Like the blue-burning match blowing over the surface of
some drunk girl's sweet, flaming party drink. Happy
birthday. Lucky

coin rubbed away to nothing, turned back into invisibility.
Back into its first atomic energy. Both

lost forever now and all around me. I've
rendered it, it seems, back into its
first longing—to keep

safe the loved ones on the plane, or on the freeway, or
strapped to the gurney, opened for the surgery, wheeled
into the lobby, being

screened for the journey, or stamped with the date
at the entrance to the pool, the portal, the night club, or

any spot where one might pull to the curb, drop
off a soft target, kiss it, make
with it a plan to fetch it later—

unbloodied, still breathing, in no hurry. This
talisman with no magic. I've made it for you

out of your own flesh, teeth, hair.

Two Gardens

1.

In this one, the great man's statue lies face down in the grass. Some butterflies. In that one, a dish made out of bone sliced so thin that, held to the sun, it disappears—because you can't hold a circle of light in your hand.

In the mud between these gardens, there are boot prints, but crossing the boundaries, freely, too, there are hundreds of long-necked birds (pink feathers) sipping honey out of hundreds of jars that have been left out for them.

2.

In one garden, this could be a generous impulse.
In that garden it could be a trap.
Someone is a bird-watcher in this one.
Someone makes ladies' feathered hats in that.

But, it's hard to tell the gardens apart from such a distance. Still, look: There's definitely a fence between them, and its white slats appear to be painted with rosebuds from over here, although those roses look like the small, red handprints of children from here.

Suffering Song

This morning my past is a small chalk bird
in the hand
of St. Francis, but my mind

is a closetful of gadgets:
smokeless ashtray, travel-
size defibrillator. All

these wild black branches clawing
at the purple sky…

My backyard is a machine, too, see?

So, why didn't you warn me
little eyeless bird
in the palm of a saint
if you saw all this coming?

Oh, she sings to me, eyeless and mechanical:
Wind me up, you'll see.

See?

In a poor translation, Montaigne
says that we
pity those who beg for mercy, but the ones
we spare are those
who rip us to pieces
with their teeth.

Therefore, if you listen you can hear
your own child's babbling creek
in the suffering
song of every creature you eat.

True Crime

A few days after her daughter's funeral, a bouquet of white roses was delivered in a long box to her front door. A small card was stuffed among thorns and petals, which card expressed something about pain giving way eventually to peace, etcetera, in clumsy poetry.

Wrapped in tissue, without a vase, it was as if some kind of romantic gesture were being made, not just one more floral arrangement meant to be set beside the coffin of the murdered girl, but to be delivered to her resurrection.

How sugary they looked, how spun—created out of ideas a girl might clip from magazines (Elle, Cosmopolitan, Seventeen) not

grown in a garden or even a greenhouse but in some factory where lacy bras and panties were stamped and stitched by other girls, faraway, who could never leave but were not called slaves, whispering to each other across the conveyor belt before before being shipped off in hot-pink plastic to some imaginary shopping mall in a country made of imagination.

She thought how her daughter would have liked these roses best of all, before she saw—

A beetle, neon green, the size of a pencil eraser or a beauty mark, clawing itself out of the center of a daydream, like a girl being chased through a forest, pursued by

an inspiration,
a man with a knife,
and a bouquet.

For a Few Minutes, Once

I felt briefly sure that there were two of me. Extra arms. Extra
everything. For instance, sensations. I

heard echoes echoing me. And all my fears seemed to be

also my freedoms—
being duplicated somewhere, rapidly, in some factory, as if
by some

supernatural machine.

Or perhaps by a completely
ordinary machine. Like

a change-machine, a war-machine, a snow-in-the-deep-blue-of-
evening-machine.

I could
somehow drive my car while
also riding my bike. I could walk a tight-rope between
two canyons while sailing over myself, walking a tightrope. As

a jet's silver crucifix in the sky. Or, snagged in electrical
wires, a kite. I was living my life
a second time
for the first time in my life, understanding that I
had already lived a long time before I realized
I was old enough by then to have been

my own mother when my mother died.

Nine Trials

1) A man on the sidewalk grabs his crotch just as a woman passes in a cab.

2) A girl in the passenger seat of a car is being driven by a friend who's talking on her iPhone. She knows she's going to die.

3) A very ordinary husband tells his wife about the ghost of a Civil War soldier he saw long ago. She knows it can't be true, but she also knows he isn't lying.

4) Woman on a train. Crude man beside her talks about her pussy before he starts to cry.

5) Girl with two boys in a crawl space. Stoned. They claim she brought them down here, so why, now that they want to get out, can't she find the door?

6) A newly married couple buys a pink house from an elderly woman. The husband says, years later, that he's never been able to sleep in the house, and his wife understands, suddenly, that by never he means never.

7) Woman meets her husband's best friend in a motel, clandestinely. He's exactly like her husband.

8) Woman married to a Vietnam veteran. His friend from the war visits, never leaves.

9) Man says he sees Jesus on the side of his tool shed, calls all the neighbors over, who also see it. The only one who can't see Jesus, although she tries and tries, is the man's wife.

The Beautiful Hand

Never underestimate the devotion
of a God who gives birth in darkness
to his own likeness

by thought alone. You

were loved wildly before you even had time to open your eyes.

But now you can never catch up.
And that's the problem.
The gifts pile up, along

with the thank you notes you never wrote, or
wrote but never sent

to the parents
who adored you, to the friend
who cheated you, to the lover
on whom you cheated, to

the magician who thought he'd tricked you as he stood

on a stage in a puddle of his assistant's blood
for your entertainment only. Only
out of love. Like the ocean

into which you should have been
more grateful
as you waded. It was every bit
as alive as you
were then, with its

purgatory of jellyfish, all
cloud and flesh and forgotten names—
passing between your legs

Rescue Annie

As silence I carry inside myself wet, white ashes. Smothered
school bells. Swans at the bottom of the well.
Thunder under a mountain of rain-soaked party dresses. The un-
performed caesarean section. The small town slumbering
under an avalanche. The sound
of the struggle ending without a sound.
Unrequited love.
Fish full of water.
Bird full of feathers. Mine, the most-kissed face in the world.

"Resusci Annie" is a training mannequin used for teaching CPR to emergency workers and members of the general public...(Her) face is based on L'Inconnue de la Seine, the death mask of an unidentified young woman reputed to have drowned in the River Seine in the late 1880s.

The Time Machine

My mother begged me: Please, please, study
stenography...

Without it
I would have no future, and this

is the future that was lost in time to me

having scoffed at her, refusing
to learn the only skill I'd ever need, the one

I will associate forever now with loss, with her
bald head, her wig, a world
already gone
by the time we had this argument, while
our walls stayed slathered in its pale green.

While we
wore its sweater sets. While we
giddily picked the pineapple
off our hams with toothpicks. Now

I'm lost somewhere between
1937
and 1973. My

time machine, blown off course, just
as my mother knew it would be.

Oh, Mama: forget about me.
You don't have to forgive
me, but know this, please:

I am
the Stenographer now.

I am
the Secretary you wanted me to be. I am

the girl who gained the expertise you
knew some day some man would need.

Too late, maybe.
(Evening.)
I'm sick, I think.
You're dead.
I'm weak.

And now I'm going to tell you
a little secret.
Get out your pen and steno-pad, and sit
down across from me.

Ready?

The grieving:

It never ends.

You learn a million
tricks, memorize
the symbols &
practice the techniques

and still you wake up every morning
lost inside your
lost machine. Confused, but always
on a journey.

 Disordered.

Cut short.

Still moving.

Keep speaking
Mama.
Please.
I'm taking it down
so quickly, so

quickly, even (perhaps especially)

when I appear

not to be.

I do this naturally.

See? In the end, no

training was needed.

None at all.

None at all.

I taught myself so well.

It's all I can do now.

Please

Anyone here who has ever stolen a ring from the finger of a corpse, raise your hand. All who have lusted burningly in your heart for a bird, please stand. (Deep in this thing, compressed, is another thing. It has no name. *Good-bye,* it sings, *to the oppressive reign of shame.*)

All who have, anonymous behind the wheel on a highway through Montana late at night, driven another vehicle off the road and just kept driving—please, call out your name. (This is the keyhole filled with light, like glory, because the room is dark and someone bolted the door and there are more rule books here than players when it comes to the game...)

If you have ever tossed a cigarette into a forest because it was dry...or torn a single month from an elderly woman's calendar (maybe June) then insisted there was no such month, shaking your head sadly and saying, "I'm just so sorry you're so confused," *tell us your story.*

For we, for we, for we—

For we
are so ordinary here—
twisting, twisting, in our nooses made of horror.

My First Mistress

My first mistress was a mirror.
She was thin as winter, and an heiress.
When I smiled at her, she smiled, and when

I grimaced, she grimaced. And when
I cried, she turned my tears to silvered
strangers in the distance.

My shining party dress inside her.
My staggering drunkenness.

And when I slipped on a new pair of shoes
and fell down wearing them. Black-
eyed, and rising up again. And when

they took off my breasts: Then
she became the surface without expression
that let me stare, and never said, "What

do you think you're staring at in there?"
Instead, she polished
my face softly with a cloth, and when

I screamed at her that I was dying, and when
I turned my back on her while she was crying

she just
reminded me, quietly, to please
remember to turn off the light.

acknowledgements

The Academy of American Poets: "The Time Machine"

The American Literary Review: "A Girl's Guide to Color"

Ghost Town: "My First Mistress"

Gulf Coast: "Suffering Song"

The Journal: "The Whole Point"

The Michigan Quarterly Review: "His Secret," "Beautiful Classmate from the Past," "True Crime," "The Nose"

Plume: "The Beautiful Hand"

Poetry: "Talisman"

Deep gratitude goes to Taylor D. Waring, Christopher Howell, and Willow Springs Books for helping me with these poems, and this collection.

acme poem company

Willow Springs Books is a small literary press housed in Eastern Washington University's MFA program in Spokane, Washington. Its annual chapbook series selects and publishes contemporary surrealist poetry under the auspices of the Acme Poem Company.

previous collections

Tooth & Shoe, Heikki Huotari
dark acre, Canese Jarboe
Black Postcards, Michael McGriff
The 9-Day Queen Gets Lost On Her Way to the Execution, Karyna McGlynn
Startle Pattern, Larissa Szporluk
Drunk on Salt, James Nolan
You Won't Need That, Robert Gregory
Gnawing on a Thin Man, Ray Amarosi
No Time for Dancing, Adam Hammer

For a complete list of selections from Willow Springs Books and ordering information, visit www.willowspringsbooks.org.

Willow Springs Books staff who contributed to this chapbook are:

Catie Feldman, Elizabeth Patrick, Jordan Dunn, Kari Rueckert, Cassandra Bruner, and Taylor D. Waring

Laura Kasischke has published eleven collections of poetry (most recently Where Now: New & Selected Poems, Copper Canyon Press, 2017) as well as nine novels and a collection of short fiction. She has received the National Book Critics Circle Award for Poetry, among other honors. She lives in Chelsea, Michigan, and teaches in the Residential College and the English Department, where she is the Theodore Roethke Distinguished University Professor.